THE BEST GIFT IS LOVE

THE BEST GIFT IS LOVE

Meditations by Mother Teresa

❖ ❖ ❖

Compiled and Edited by
Sean-Patrick Lovett

CHARIS

Servant Publications
Ann Arbor, Michigan

First published in both Italian and English in 1982
by Libreria Editrice Vaticana in Vatican City.

Published in the United States of America in English in 1993 by
Servant Publications
P.O. Box 8617
Ann Arbor, Michigan 48107

Cover design by Michael Andaloro
Cover photo copyright Rick Friedman/ Black Star
Text design by K. Kelly Bonar

02 03 10 9

Printed in the United States of America
ISBN 0-89283-814-0

Library of Congress Cataloging-in-Publication Data
Teresa, Mother, 1910–
    [Via all'amore. English]
    The best gift is love : meditations / by Mother Teresa :
compiled and edited by Sean-Patrick Lovett.
        p. 110 cm
    ISBN 0-89283-814-0
    1. Meditations. I. Lovett, Sean-Patrick. II. Title.
    BX2185.T4713 1993
242—dc20
                                                    92-42958

Dear Sean,
Keep the joy of loving
        Jesus
in your heart and share
this joy with all you meet
through your writing.
        God bless you
        M. Teresa, M.C.
        5/5/82

Contents

———

"Where there is great love, there are always great miracles."

———

INTRODUCTION

✦ ✦ ✦

Love–a word that seems utterly inseparable from the name of Mother Teresa. Her way of life is so much a way of love that she stands for the whole world as a symbol for all that is good and compassionate in humanity. By her very existence she provides an alternative to the awfulness of a confused world, holding out in her two consoling hands the irreplaceable cornerstones of faith and love. She represents the very elements for which all of humanity yearns: light and love, strength, peace and joy. Television documentaries have celebrated her, numerous articles and books have described her practical dedication to the poorest of the poor. Yet, somehow, no amount of documentation or description is ever enough to lead one to a full appreciation of who Mother Teresa of Calcutta really is, or how she can accomplish all she does–unless one first understands the way she loves.

I certainly never understood, even though I had been meeting with Mother Teresa over a period of four years; I had not only seen the documentaries and read all the books, but had interviewed her myself on several occasions. The impression I was inevitably left with was of trying to reach something which was essentially outside my experience. The only solution would be to "see for myself"–to hear, taste, smell and touch this reality which Mother Teresa herself always refers to as simply "the work."

And so I went to Calcutta. I stood in the midst of that "city of dreadful night" and listened to the last straining breaths of the dying. I ate the food of the poor and tasted the dry dust in my mouth. I held an aborted baby in my hand and felt it struggle to live. I watched a woman give birth amid the stench and filth of a crowded street where thousands of people live, love, work, sleep and die. I visited the place where the lepers are taken care of–where in some cases they are cured, where in all cases they are loved. And there–I understood.

It was not a slow dawning of realization. It came suddenly, unexpectedly, and I sat beside a leprosy patient, holding his hand.

When I left Mother Teresa that morning, she had told me quite explicitly, knowing where I was going: "Don't go and use your eyes only–use your hands as well!" I was horrified at the thought, but then I never expected to find what I did.

It is always difficult to describe a really deep emotional experience–the few definitive points in our lives are better passed without words. There is the danger that the moment we try to give it expression, we diminish the experience, we reduce it to cliché, we lapse into sentimentality.

How to describe, then, this sensation of holding out

your hands to a leper, of seeing the joy in his eyes, of experiencing the response of his love? How to describe the feeling of being totally emptied and filled at the same time—drained of self to the point where you no longer see the disfigured human being before you, and filled with a love which is so pure, so overpowering, that as you place your hand in his you really feel you are touching the living body of Jesus...?

At the entrance to the leprosarium there is a small notice which reads:

Where there is great love,
There are always great miracles.

The more I understood Mother Teresa's way of love, the more I saw and experienced great miracles: wherever she took me in Calcutta—to the house for dying destitutes, to the home for abandoned babies, or to the leper colony. Her love is so utterly selfless, so pure, so vast—a love which embraces the whole of humanity, in the form of a tiny aborted baby, or in the mutilated figure of a leper. For Mother Teresa they are one and the same thing: they are Jesus. In loving and touching them (and for her that human contact is essential to complete the love) we are giving our hands and our hearts to Jesus.

This book is an attempt to share the experiences of what it is like to know Mother Teresa of Calcutta. The meditations contained in it are a synthesis of the many things she has said to me over the four years I have known her. They provide a synopsis of her thoughts, her philosophy, her way of life, her way of love....

Sean-Patrick Lovett
Rome 1982

Mother Teresa in a moment of prayer

―――――

Happy
the pure in heart,
they shall see
God.

Matthew 5:8

―――――

ONE

PURITY

❖ ❖ ❖

The pure heart is a heart that is free,
free to give,
to love until it hurts.
The pure heart is a heart that serves,
that loves God with undivided love.

The pure heart can easily see Christ
in the hungry,
in the naked,
in the homeless,

in the lonely,
in the unwanted,
in the unloved,
in the leper,
in the alcoholic,
in the man lying in the street–
unwanted, unloved, uncared for,
hungry....
He is not hungry for lack of a piece of bread,
he is hungry for love....
He is not naked just for lack of a piece of cloth,
he is naked because he has been stripped of human
    dignity...
He is not homeless just because he lacks a small house
to live in,
his homelessness comes from being abandoned by all...
unwanted, unloved, uncared for,
neglected....
He has forgotten the meaning of human love,

*The famed missionary prays at the dedication of a new house
for her Missionaries of Charity in Washington, D.C.,
which will care for AIDS patients*

human joy,
human touch.

To be able to see Christ in the distressing disguise of
these, our brothers and sisters,
we need a pure heart…
a pure heart is free to serve,
a pure heart is free to love…
and these, the poor, our brothers and sisters,
are the hope of salvation for mankind,
for at the hour of our death we are going to be judged
according to what we have done to them!
If we have had the pure eyes to see Christ
in the distressing disguise of the poor.…
Just as we need pure eyes to see Him
in the appearance of bread,
we need pure eyes to see Him
in the distressing disguise of the poor…

the suffering,
the unwanted,
the unloved,
those people society has discarded as useless–
they are Jesus.

Mother Teresa's inimitable smile cheers our hearts.

———

*If you keep my commandments, you
will live remain in my love,
just as I have kept
my Father's commandments
and remain in his love.
I have told you this
so that my own joy may be in you and
your joy be complete.*

John 15:10–11

———

Joy

❖ ❖ ❖

Naturally our joy will be complete
if we remain in His love—
for His love is personal,
intimate,
real,
living,
delicate,
faithful love.

When Jesus was born,
the angels proclaimed His coming with joy:

"… Rejoice…!"
Joy, because Jesus has been born.
The shepherds and everyone around Jesus
seemed to radiate joy,
the joy Jesus Himself said He had come to give:

———

"… that my joy may be complete in you.…"
St. Paul speaks often of that joy,
and at Baptism the priest tells the baptized soul:
"… go and serve the Church with joy.…"

A joyful heart is like a sunshine of God's love,
the hope of eternal happiness,
a burning flame of God.
So if we allow Him to live His life in us,
we will experience that joy.
And if we pray,
we will become that sunshine of God's love—
in our own home,
the place where we live,
and in the world at large.

The world today is hungry
for the joy that comes from a pure heart,
for a pure heart can see God.

Mother Teresa receives Communion from Pope John Paul II at a Mass for Peace in Quezon City, Philippines.

---

*I am the bread of life.
He who comes to me
will never be hungry;
he who believes in me
will never thirst.*

John 6:35

THREE

HUNGER

✦ ✦ ✦

That is a great truth:
whoever eats His Flesh and drinks His Blood
will never hunger.
That is why Jesus made Himself
"Bread of Life"—
to satisfy our hunger for God,
our hunger for love,
for Divine love,
that everlasting love,
that infinite love....

And as if that were not enough for Him,
He too made Himself the hungry one,
so that we could satisfy His hunger for human love.

Jesus puts it so beautifully when He says:
"I was hungry and you gave me to eat;
I was naked and you clothed me;
I was sick and you took care of me;
I was homeless and you took me in...."

God's hunger for human love,
for human care,
for human touch,
for that human joy of loving and touching—
that is why He became man:
to be able to be loved by you and by me.

Mother Teresa comforts a polio victim
at a Home for the Destitute run by her sisters
in Manila, Philippines.

With a heart of conviction, Mother Teresa addresses
a Right-to-Life Convention in Washington, D.C., in 1985.

"Do not let your hearts be troubled.
Trust in God still and trust in me.
There are many rooms
in my Father's house;
I am going now to prepare a place for you,
and after I have gone
and prepared you a place,
I shall return to take you with me;
so that where I am
you may be too."

John 14:1-3

DEATH

There is no need to fear death,
because death is nothing more than going home to God.
For me, that is the greatest development of a human life:
to die in peace with God.

We have homes for the sick and dying,
destitutes,
and it is so beautiful to see how these people,

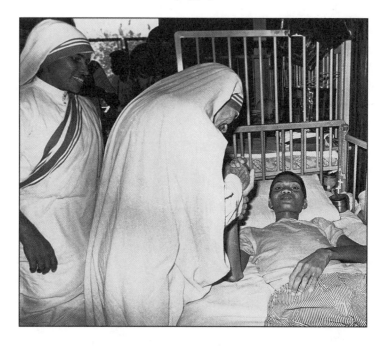

Mother Teresa listens attentively to the concerns of a sick man in a Home for the Destitute in Manila, Philippines.

who have lived such difficult lives,
die with such contentment,
with such peace–
it really is unbelievable.

We picked one of them out of a drain once
and brought him to the Home for the Dying.
I remember him saying:
"I have lived like an animal in the street,
but I am going to die like an angel–
loved and cared for...."
He had no fear.
We fear only when our conscience is not clear,
when we are afraid to face ourselves.
That is why so many people are afraid of death–
they are afraid of facing reality,
of facing self,
by looking at God.

A pure heart sees God,
and I think the poor people
live very much in the presence of God,
that is why they have no fear,
that is why they meet death with happiness.
I find that our people in the Homes for the Dying,
our lepers and so on,
their happiness at death
is not due to their being released from suffering,
it is because they are truly at peace–
a peace which shines through in their faces.
Although thousands of people die in our Homes each year,
I have never yet seen anybody die in distress,
or in despair,
or restless…
they simply go home to God.

*During the papal visit of February, 1986, Pope John Paul II and
Mother Teresa pray for those who had recently died
in her home for the dying in Calcutta.*

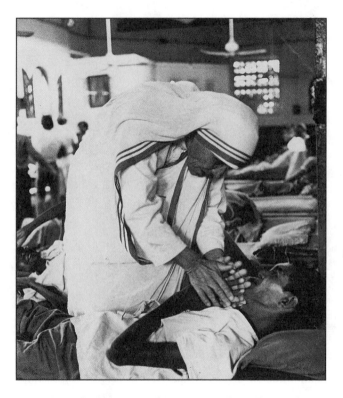

Mother Teresa comforts a man who is dying

———

*"A man can have no greater love
than to lay down his life for his friends.
You are my friends,
if you do what I command you....
I call you friends,
because I have made known to you
everything I have learnt
from my Father."*

John 15:13–15

———

FIVE

FRIENDSHIP

No one can make a better friend than Jesus—
because His love is so humble
and so tender....

The true way
and the sure way to friendship
is through humility—
being open to each other,
accepting each other just as we are,
knowing each other.

*After pouring herself out in love and service of others,
an exhausted Mother Teresa pauses for a moment of prayer.*

That knowledge leads to great love,
and love leads to great service,
giving to each other.
For me, that is friendship–
that knowing each other,
accepting each other just as we are,
so that we can love one another
and so fulfill the words of Jesus:

"Love one another as I have loved you–
as the Father has loved me."

How did the Father love Him?
by giving Him–
He gave Him up…
and Jesus loved me by giving Himself to me…
therefore, I too must love my friend by giving myself to him.
That means by being completely open to him,

openness and humility are the same thing,
and that is why Jesus can love with such great love–
because He has humbled Himself by becoming one of us,
so that we might love Him
as He has loved us.

A woman of deep faith, Mother Teresa joins in prayer with her Missionaries of Charity.

The doors were closed, but Jesus came in and stood among them. "Peace be with you," he said. Then he spoke to Thomas, "Put your finger here; look, there are my hands. Give me your hand; put it into my side. Doubt no longer but believe."

Thomas replied, "My Lord and my God!"

Jesus said to him: "You believe because you can see me. Happy are those who have not seen and yet believe."

John 20:26–29

SIX

FAITH

One of the most beautiful
and one of the most encouraging passages in the Gospel–
those words of Jesus regarding Faith:
"Happy are those who have not seen and yet believe."

The fruit of prayer is Faith.
If we pray,
then we will believe.
If we believe,
then we will love–

*Mother Teresa and members of her Order
kneel in daily prayer
at their headquarters in Calcutta, India.*

because the fruit of Faith is love,
and the fruit of love is service.
Similarly, if we want to deepen our Faith,
we must deepen our oneness with Christ.

Without seeing Him
we pray to Him,
we turn to Him,
we cling to Him,
we love Him
without seeing Him.

Faith
is the most beautiful gift God can give to a human being–
to believe that He *IS*,
and that Christ *IS*…
God from God,
Love from Love,
true God from true God,

begotten, not made;
one in substance with the Father,
by whom all things were made....

And yet He became so small,
He became a human being like us,
to make it possible for us to believe.
To increase our Faith
He made Himself the Bread of Life–
even a child can break that Bread,
even a child can eat that Bread.
This is humility in the action of Faith,
and Faith in the action of humility.

We can understand the majesty of God,
it is very difficult to understand the humility of God.
That is why we need to pray–
to be able to believe.

Mother Teresa leads in prayer while addressing a large crowd.

Mother Teresa joins in song at the opening of a new home for old people and abandoned children at Addis Ababa, Ethiopia.

Now once he was in a certain place praying, and when he had finished one of his disciples said, "Lord, teach us to pray, just as John taught his disciples."

He said this to them, "Say this when you pray:

Father, may your name be held holy,
your kingdom come;
give us each day our daily bread,
and forgive us our sins,
for we ourselves forgive each one who is in debt
  to us.
And do not put us to the test."

Luke 11:1–4

SEVEN

PRAYER

✧ ✧ ✧

Talk to God.
Just let Jesus pray in you.

To be able to pray
we need silence–
because God speaks to us in the silence of the heart,
and we reply from the fullness of the heart.
God speaking in the silence of our heart,
we replying in the fullness of our heart–
these two together
make prayer.

Mother Teresa enters a center of prayer and ministry to the poor run by her Order in Brooklyn, New York.

The fruit of prayer is always deepening of Faith,
and Faith cannot exist by itself–
it has to transform itself into love.
Love completes Faith.
Faith completes love,
When we really love,
we naturally want to love others–
and that loving others is our love for God in action.
That is why prayer is so important,
even for my own Sisters and our way of life.
To be able to live a life of complete belonging to Christ,
we need that continual oneness with Christ,
in order to go on putting our love for Christ into action
through the service of the poorest of the poor.

Everything begins with prayer–
spending a little time on our knees....
If all the world's rulers and leaders
would spend a little time on their knees before God,
I believe we would have a better world.

If all the world's families
would spend a little time together in prayer,
I believe we would have peace in the world.
Just as love begins at home,
so peace begins at home—
when a family is united through prayer.

So talk to God,
let Jesus pray in you…
and if you really belong totally to Him,
in whatever kind of life He has put you,
if you just let Him pray in you—
live His life in you—
then that oneness with Christ
is prayer.

Prayer means talking to God.
He is my Father.
Jesus is my all.

*Mother Teresa prays with a group of young people
at St. Francis of Assisi Church in Hong Kong.*

Mother Teresa expressing the joy and love of the Lord.

———

Everyone moved by the spirit
is a son of God.
The spirit you received is not
the spirit of slaves bringing fear
into your lives again;
it is the spirit of sons,
and it makes you cry out
"Abba, Father!"

Romans 8:14–15

———

EIGHT

GOD–
OUR FATHER

❖ ❖ ❖

The Father–
the most beautiful gift that Jesus gave us on earth.
He said it to Philip:
"To have seen me is to have seen the Father....
I am in the Father and the Father is in me...."

And when He taught us to pray, He said:
"Say this when you pray:
'Our Father'...

Mother Teresa holds the hand of the Holy Father during his visit to India in February of 1986

your Father and my Father…
'Our Father'…"

And on another occasion He told us:
"Love one another,
as I have loved you…
As the Father has loved me,
so I have loved you…."

Jesus was so sure of His Father's love for Him,
and for His love for His Father,
that all the time He wanted to make us realize
how much the Father loves us too.
God loves us tenderly with a love He has proved…
and so tender is His love
that He will never force Himself on us–
God will never disturb a soul,
rather, He draws a soul,
God lifts a soul,

and then fills it with His love.
God cannot fill what is already full though,
and that is why we need to be empty
for Him to be able to fill us.
That is why, if we want to feel His presence,
we need a pure heart–
for a pure heart can see God–
and if we see God
then that's the beginning of love:
our love for God
and God's love for us.

Today God loves the world through us,
just as before He proved His love for the world
by giving His Son
to Mary the most pure…
and she went "in haste" to give Him to others.
And He loved us so much
He made Himself the Bread of Life.

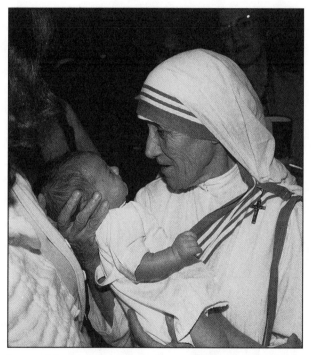

While attending a meeting of the American Family Life Institute in Washington, D.C., Mother Teresa cradles a six-week-old infant.

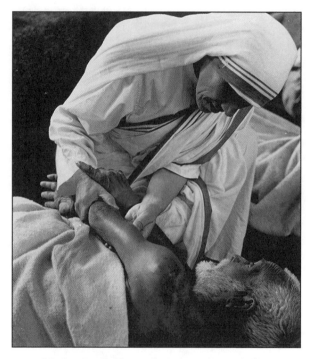

*Mother Teresa shows the compassion of Christ
to a sick, elderly man.*

And we too must love,
we too must give until it hurts.

Today God loves the world through us,
He keeps on loving the world
by sending us into the world–
to be His love,
His compassion.

*Ever on the go, Mother Teresa spends a moment
with a journalist on the airport tarmac.*

*In those days Mary arose and went with
haste into the hill country, to a city of Judah,
and she entered the house of Zechariah
and greeted Elizabeth. And when Elizabeth
heard the greeting of Mary,
the babe leaped in her womb;
and Elizabeth was filled with the Holy Spirit
and she exclaimed with a loud cry,
"Blessed are you among women,
and blessed is the fruit of your womb!"*

Luke 1:39–42

NINE

MARY–
OUR MOTHER

❖ ❖ ❖

Mary–
God's most beautiful gift to the human race.

The moment Jesus came into her life
she was "full of grace"–
and immediately she went "with haste" to give Him to others.
The fruit of her oneness with Christ,
the fruit of her prayer,
the fruit of her total surrender to God
by saying:

"Behold, I am the handmaid of the Lord;
let it be done to me according to your word...."

The fruit of her oneness with God's will
was her longing and desire to give Him to others–
so she went "with haste" to do this,
the humble work of a handmaid...
and that is just what God expects from you and from me.

When we eat the Bread of Life
we too are full of God,
full of Jesus....
Do we really take Him "with haste" to others?
The people with whom we come in contact–
in our home,
in the place where we work–
can they really see Jesus in us?
Does the light of Jesus shine in us
and through us
to others?

*Mother Teresa passes a battery of photographers
as she arrives at the Vatican for a series of meetings.*

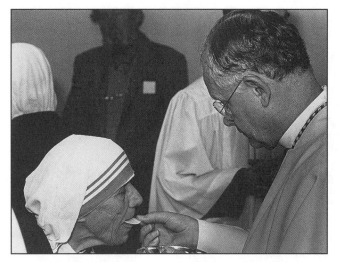

It should.
Because the same Jesus who came into Mary's womb
comes to us in Holy Communion,
and we too, like her, must go "with haste"
to give Him to others.
That is why we should ask her always:

_____

"Mary–
give us your heart
so beautiful,
so pure,
so immaculate,
your heart so full of love and humility,
that we may be able to receive and carry Jesus,
as you received and carried Him,
to others.
You are a cause of joy to us
because you gave us Jesus–
help us to be a cause of joy to others,
giving only Jesus
to all those with whom we come in contact."

Today more than ever before
people are hungry for Jesus–
and He is the only answer,
if we really want peace in the world.

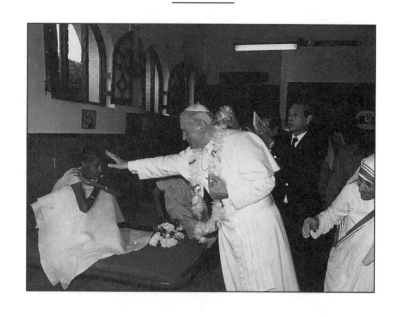

*During his papal visit of February, 1986, to India,
the Pope blesses a man
in one of Mother Teresa's homes.*

Jesus was left alone with the woman,
who remained standing there.
He looked up and said,
"Woman, where are they?
Has no one condemned you?"
"No one, sir," she replied.
"Neither do I condemn you," said Jesus,
"Go away, and don't sin any more."

John 8:9–11

TEN

FORGIVENESS

✦ ✦ ✦

Jesus is able to forgive so much
because He loves so much.
Great love can forgive great sin.

As it is for Jesus so it must be for us–
if we really want to forgive
we must really love.

Then too, it is not enough just to forgive—
we must also forget…
and to be able to forget
we need humility.
We need deep humility
to be able to forget the hurt,
as we need deep love
to be able to forgive.
Humility and love complete that forgiveness,
because the fruit of forgiveness
is to forget the hurt.
It is so much easier to forgive than to forget,
but if we do not forget
then we have not forgiven.

With Jesus it is always complete:
"Go away and don't sin any more."
It is finished.
In every confession He shows us that same forgiveness—

Mother Teresa speaks to a crowd of Jesus' love and forgivness which is extended to all.

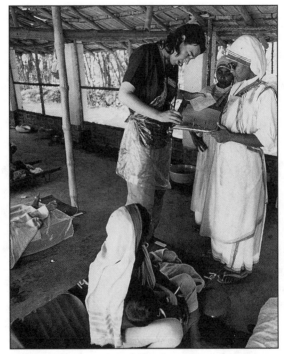

*Some Missionaries of Charity assist a doctor in
a field hospital, a sign of God's mercy extended to all.*

He stoops down and takes away our sins
through the absolution that the priest gives us.
The words of the priest
and the hands of the priest in absolution
take away our sin,
wash away every stain from our lives–
forgiving,
forgetting.

I remember finding a man in a sewer,
and the Sisters took him and cleaned him,
cared for him,
and he never once said a word.
After two days he finally spoke to the Sisters and said:
"You have brought God into my life–bring a priest also."
The Sisters went and brought a priest,
and the man made his confession
for the first time in sixty years.

Next morning he died.
It was such a wonderful manifestation of God's greatness
and the power He has given
to the words and hands of the priest.
God had come into that man's life,
but the connection had to be made
through the power God has given to the priest.

The greatness of the priestly vocation:
to take away sin,
to wash away every stain from our lives–
forgiving,
forgetting.

*Mother Teresa and Father Robert P. Hupp,
director of Boys Town, are surrounded by students
during her visit to the center for homeless boys in Nebraska.*

*Mother Teresa speaks out for
the poor and suffering in our world.*

*As Jesus went along, He saw a man
who had been blind from birth.
His disciples asked him:
"Master, who sinned, this man or his
parents, for him to have been born blind?"
"Neither he nor his parents sinned,"
Jesus answered, "He was born blind
so that the works of God
might be displayed in him."*

John 9:1–3

ELEVEN

SUFFERING

I wonder what the world would be like
if there were not innocent people
making reparation for us all...?

Today the passion of Christ is being relived
in the lives of those who suffer.
To accept that suffering is a gift of God.

Suffering is not a punishment.
God does not punish.

*Mother Teresa, a sign of the joy of the Lord
in our world of suffering*

Suffering is a gift–
though,
like all gifts,
it depends on how we receive it.
And that is why we need a pure heart–
to see the hand of God,
to feel the hand of God,
to recognize the gift of God
in our suffering.

Suffering is not a punishment.
Jesus does not punish.
Suffering is a sign–
a sign
that we have come so close
to Jesus on the cross,
that He can kiss us,
show that He is in love with us,

by giving us an opportunity to share
in His passion.

In our Home for the Dying
it is so beautiful to see
people who are joyful,
people who are lovable,
people who are at peace,
in spite of terrible suffering.

Suffering is not a punishment,
not a fruit of sin,
it is a gift of God.
He allows us to share in His suffering
and to make up for the sins of the world.

*Mother Teresa prays for God's mercy and compassion,
especially for those who experience terrible suffering in our world*

Mother Teresa addresses an American Family Institute symposium in Washington, D.C.

———

*Husbands should love their wives
just as Christ loved the Church…
each one of you must love his wife
as he loves himself;
and let every wife respect her husband.
Children, be obedient to your parents
in the Lord—that is your duty.…
And parents,
never drive your children to resentment.*

Ephesians 5:25, 33; 6:1, 4

———

TWELVE

THE FAMILY

✦ ✦ ✦

A father and mother—
by loving their children,
by loving one another,
they are loving God.

But just as love and peace begin at home,
so do disturbance and sadness also begin at home—
when a family is not united.

The family that prays together, stays together.
But more and more we see
that families are not staying together,
and this is the greatest destroyer of peace in the world.

If there is so much disturbance in the world today,
if there is so much sadness,
so much killing
and anxiety,
it is because the family is no longer united...
father against mother,
children against children...
a mother committing a murder in her own womb,
a mother who is afraid of her own child,
afraid to have to love one more child,
so afraid that she must kill that child–
the child must die so that she may live,
so that she may be free.
If a mother can kill her own child,
what is there to stop others from killing one another?

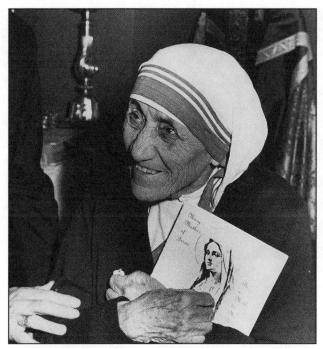

*Mother Teresa clutches an image of the Blessed Mother,
whose prayers she frequently invokes for families.*

Mother Teresa embraces a nine-month-old Swiss baby
on a visit to Hong Kong.

If today there is so much suffering in the world,
so much pain,
it is because the child–
the unborn child,
the innocent child–
is unwanted, unloved, uncared for.

I think the best gift we can give to any child
is to make that child feel
wanted, loved, cared for–
because that child is the greatest gift of God
to the family,
to the nation,
to the world.
Because that child is the Life of God,
created for greater things,
in the image of God–
to love
and to be loved.

President Ronald Reagan presented the Medal of Freedom to Mother Teresa in 1985.

———

"You did not choose me,
no, I chose you;
and I commissioned you
to go out and to bear fruit,
fruit that will last."

John 15:16

———

THIRTEEN

VOCATION

❖ ❖ ❖

Vocation is simply a call to belong totally to Christ,
with the conviction that nothing can separate me
from His love.

Vocation is an invitation to be in love with God
and to prove that love.

How do I love God?
How do I prove my love for God?
By doing beautifully the work I have been given to do,
by doing simply that which God has entrusted to me,

in whatever form it may take.
Like my Sisters who take vows–
in full reality they become the spouse of Jesus crucified–
and that is their vocation:
to love Christ with undivided love
in chastity,
in true freedom of poverty,
in total surrender to obedience,

and in whole-hearted free service to the poorest of the poor.
They prove their love for God
by putting that love in a living action.

So whatever the work with which you have been entrusted–
as a religious,
as a layperson–
it is a means for you to put your love for God
in a living action,
in an action of love....
Every time you smile at someone,
it is an action of love,
a gift to that person,
a beautiful thing....

So if I want to know how much I love Christ,
if I want to know if I am really in love with God,
then I have only to look at how I do the work
He has entrusted to me–
how much love I put into the doing of that work.

You see, it is not the work in itself that is our vocation—
our vocation is to belong totally to Jesus,
with the conviction that nothing can separate us from
His love.

It is not what we are doing,
or how much we are doing,
but rather,
how much love we are putting in the doing
of that work entrusted to us.

What you are doing
I may not be able to do....
What I am doing
you may not be able to do....
But all of us together
are doing
something beautiful for God.

"… My prayer for you is that you may grow in holiness
through love for one another—for where there is love,
there is peace…. And if there is peace, there is joy.
So keep the joy of loving one another in your hearts,
and share this joy with all you meet…."

God bless you
Mc Teresa mc

ACKNOWLEDGMENTS

Photos courtesy of the following:

ONE
p. 14, CNS, (Catholic News Service)/KNA.
p. 19, CNS/Michael Hoyt.

TWO
p. 22, UPI/Bettmann Archives.
p. 26, UPI/Bettmann Archives.

THREE
p. 28, CNS/Arturo Mari.
p. 33, UPI/Bettmann Archives.

FOUR
p. 34, UPI/Bettmann Archives.
p. 38, UPI/Bettmann Archives.
p. 41, CNS/Arturo Mari.

FIVE

p. 42,   CNS/KNA.

p. 46,   CNS/Michael Hoyt.

SIX

p. 50,   CNS/Michael Hoyt.

p. 54,   UPI/Bettmann Archives.

p. 57,   CNS/Michael Hoyt.

SEVEN

p. 58,   CNS/Michael Hoyt.

p. 62,   CNS/KNA.

p. 65,   Reuters/Bettmann Archives.

EIGHT

p. 66,   CNS/Michael Hoyt.

p. 70,   Reuters/Bettmann Archives.

p. 73,   UPI/Bettmann Archives.

p. 74,   CNS/KNA.

NINE

p. 76,   CNS/KNA.

p. 81,   UPI/Bettmann Archives.

p. 82,   CNS/Michael Hoyt.

TEN

p. 84,   CNS/Arturo Mari.

p. 89,   CNS/Michael Hoyt.

p. 90,   CNS/KNA.

p. 93,   Religious News Service Photo.

ELEVEN

p. 94,   CNS/James Baco.

p. 98,   CNS/Michael Hoyt.

p. 101,   CNS/Michael Hoyt.

TWELVE

p. 102,   CNS/Tom Kane.

p. 107,   CNS/Michael Hoyt.

p. 108,   Reuters/Bettmann Archives.

THIRTEEN

p. 110,   UPI/Bettmann Archives.

p. 114,   CNS/Michael Hoyt.

ANOTHER BOOK OF INTEREST FROM SERVANT PUBLICATIONS

Blessed Are You:
Mother Teresa and the Beatitudes
Prepared by Eileen Egan and
Kathleen Egan, O.S.B.

Here are Mother Teresa's reflections on the beatitudes, pointing to the heart of the gospel, as a sign of contradiction to the world and a source of spiritual freedom for all who follow Jesus. A moving black-and-white photo of Mother Teresa living one of the beatitudes opens each chapter. Each chapter then includes reflections by Mother Teresa on the beatitude, an opening meditation by Eileen and Kathleen Egan, and a closing sketch of Mother Teresa and her Sisters, the Missionaries of Charity, living the beatitude and bringing Jesus' love into the farthest corners of the world.   *hardcover,* **$10.99**